Unless otherwise identified, all scripture quotations are taken from the King James Version of the Holy Bible. Scripture quotations marked NIV are taken from the New International Version of the bible. Scripture quotations marked NKJV are taken from the New King James Version. All Hebrew and Greek references are taken from The New Strong's Exhaustive Concordance of the bible

Monarch Publications, LLC books may be purchased in bulk for educational, business, fundraising or sales promotional use. For more information, please email monarchpublicationsllc@yahoo.com

Brown, Valerie 2009

Flowing in the Spirit Christian Poems a la carte / By Valerie Brown

ISBN 978-0-578-03673-1

Front Cover Design Concept by Ayana Johnson
Front and back cover designed by Timothy Hawkins

Warning—Disclaimer
Every effort has been made to make this manual as complete and as accurate as possible. However, there may be mistakes, both typographical and in content.

The author nor publisher shall have neither liability nor responsibility to any person or entity with respect to any of or damage caused, or alleged to have been caused, directly or indirectly, by the information contained in this book.

Flowing In The Spirit

Christian Poems a la carte

By Valerie Brown

SUMMARY

I began writing at age 14. At that time it was just simple words on paper, a way to release my thoughts. It was not until I began living for Christ in my early twenties that the words would take on a life of their own. I write from experience or imagine myself as someone else. It is my desire to share the words that God has given me with others to help, heal, and renew the spirit. *Flowing in the Spirit* is my first collection of heart-felt writings from the soul. It is my intent that you will sit back, relax, and enjoy each piece. Take a moment to ponder about yourself and record your thoughts on the outline provided after each piece.

"Now unto him that is able to do exceeding abundantly above all that we ask or think, according to the power that worketh in us".

Ephesians 3:20 KJV

DEDICATION

This book is dedicated to my father, **Robert Curry Sr**.
He passed away January 11, 1998. He always encouraged me to make a difference in my life. He felt my life should have meaning and purpose. I love you, Daddy.

I also dedicate this book to my mother, **Janniece Curry**.
You are a very loving and caring woman. Thank you for instilling morals and values in me. You were healed from cancer many years ago and I pray you will continue to live a full and productive life.

To my amazing husband, **Darrell Brown** who always strives for excellence. I am blessed to have you in my life. With you, I've learned the true meaning of love. Together we have learned how to trust God and encompass all that He has for us.

To my precious children, **Mahoghani and Darrell Jr**. Both of you have brought me great joy. May your lives, hopes and dreams be fulfilled in every way. I love you more than you'll ever know. Keep God first, and everything else will follow.

ACKNOWLEDGEMENTS

I first acknowledge my siblings; **Tiffani, Robert, David (Joby)**. Each one of you have played a significant role in my life. You have contributed in different ways. All of which help shape me into the person I am today. I pray God manifests Himself in a personal way to each of you and your children.

Also to my newest family members; **William and Nyasha, Dezhane, Star, William Jr, William III and Romeo.**
For such a time as this, you've entered into our lives and I pray God unfolds His plan in each one of us. I believe our family will become more and more special in the days that lie ahead.

Kim Walker, Angela Evans, Ms. Spear, Dodie and Terri.
You have been great friends for over 25 years. You have opened your lives and your homes to me and let me walk in. You've <u>always</u> treated me as family. Whether I was right or wrong I knew you would be honest with me. I truly believe you were placed in my life for a reason and I value the relationship we have. Your children can be proud of each one of you.

Lowanda and Sylvester Cooper. You have been there for me and my children many times. I knew I could always count on you at a moment's notice. May God give you the knowledge and wisdom to continue your walk in this life with strength and determination. Your faithfulness is a witness for Christ.

Marilyn Wyatt. She passed away December 14, 2005. She played an intricate role in my life many years ago. She took me to the book of Jeremiah and had me to read it. The deposit she made in my heart is one I'll never forget. She believed in me before I believed in myself.

Elder Stephen and Sister Marion Brown. Thank you for building the foundation of God's word in my life. It was the stability I needed to follow the path that was set before me. Thank you for your love and patience shown to me since I was a young adult. May God bless you and your family always.

My sisters in Christ:

Sister Lisa Colbert, you gave me the connection with Monarch Publications, LLC. May God bring great increase to you and your family.

Sister Ayana Johnson, thank you for the art design. You are so gifted and you have great ideas that are shown through your creativity. You have a sweet, gentle spirit and I am most appreciative for all your work. May the blessings of God overtake you and your family.

Minister Andrea Bowens-Jones, you've sacrificed much of your time into this book. My gratitude extends beyond measure. I am deeply moved by the compassion and excitement you've shown throughout this project. The fact that you were willing to commit to this touches my heart. May God make your way prosperous going in and coming out.

Acknowledging my Pastor, **George C. Evans Jr. and First Lady Minister Sandra Evans**. I appreciate you both very much. I can be assured that you will give me (and Greater Harvest Church) the uncut truth about any matter. You have a spirit of excellence and you propel me to press toward the best in every area of life. Most of all, your sermons empower me to seek God always, and to never give up. I am thankful that you are a shepherd who watches over his flock while having a sensitive ear to hear what the spirit of the Lord is saying.

Finally, thank you **Mrs. Holly Spence**. You believed in me the first day we met. It was truly a blessing that you and I connected from the beginning. Thank you for all you've done.

Dare to Believe

My enemy, who is known to mankind
Thrives on deceit and confusing the mind
I allowed him to come in and take my joy
His goal was my life - he plotted to destroy
He worked overtime on the job to see if I'd fall
He wanted my circumstances to create such a wall
Between me and my Lord, he tried for awhile
To break our fellowship and not press through the trial

One by one things fell apart - I didn't understand
It happened because I took it from God's hands
I was learning how to grow up in Christ
Becoming what God intended came with a price
In order to finish this spiritual race,
God permitted certain events to take place

He told me to focus on Him and Him alone
I was now where He wanted me - at the foot of His
throne
Crying out before Him - surrendering all of me
My soul was fighting hard to be free
My decision was final, no need to pretend
I will not live without Him - I'll endure to the end…

Table of Contents

Section I: Wake Up

Section II: Mid Day Snack

Section III: Beside Chat

Section IV: Munchies

I

Wake Up

"Arise, shine, for the light is come, and the glory of the Lord is risen upon thee".

Isaiah 60:1 KJV

"Arise!"
A wake up call

So you've been storing your treasures at heaven's gate

Consistently building while enduring the wait

Seeking His face, His direction, His plan

The essence of Christ has been holding your hand

Now it's time to voice what you believe

Be diligent in the kingdom and continue to weave

The pattern He's set before our eyes

Casting down strongholds pressing for the prize

Stand up soldier in this spiritual war

Press your way through as never before

There's a call in the land to prepare yourself strong

Plant your feet well for it won't be long!

ARISE

SAINTS

ARISE!

Reflections

My thoughts are:

_____

_____

_____

_____

_____

_____

_____

Reflections

My thoughts are:

_____

_____

_____

_____

_____

_____

_____

Reflections

My thoughts are:

_____

_____

_____

_____

_____

_____

_____

_____

Forbidden Fruit

And God formed man from the dust of the ground

Just imagine the glory - nothing like it could be found

He breathed into his nostrils making him a living soul

Come with me as we journey through this story told

There in this garden He placed man whom He formed

Out of all His creation, it was Adam He adorned

From Adams' rib came Eve, his mate for life

She was designed as his help meet - her role as wife

In this garden, God had Adam dress and keep it

Giving him this responsibility seemed to be fit

For God always does things decent and in order

Never just getting by or skimming the border

There stood trees good for food and pleasant to the sight

Sometimes good things can be wrong and

something else turns out right

God said, the tree of knowledge of good and evil -

you **cannot** have

Only obedience would have kept them on the path

The Word was spoken God couldn't lie

In the day that thou eatest thereof, thou shalt surely die

Just a bite, a juicy taste

Now a Savior had to come to redeem the human race

So you say that was then, this is now,

how does this relate?

When we choose our own way, we've sealed our own fate

How many times do we drag ourselves down

Entangled in this world that keeps us bound

When you look at a picture, it can appear to be fine

It's only when you focus in can you detect subtle lines

You might be the witness others need to see

To unlock the cage and set the captives free

"I would that you were hot or cold" lukewarm won't do

You've heard this verse before - it isn't new

Having one foot in Egypt, the other in the Promised Land

Was not what God intended in His divine plan

The world managed to filter their self-made principles in

To choke out God's Word to bring His Kingdom to an end

We say God is love, God understands, surely He'll forgive

Stop using that excuse, confess your sin and you will live.

Reflections

My thoughts are:

_____

_____

_____

_____

_____

_____

_____

Reflections

My thoughts are:

_____

_____

_____

_____

_____

_____

_____

Reflections

My thoughts are:

_____

_____

_____

_____

_____

_____

_____

_____

Have you really made Jesus Lord?

We confess He is Lord and believe He is real
But do we mean it, or is it something we feel?
We'll search through scriptures and read His word
Is it alive in our hearts or simply words we've heard?
If Jesus is who we claim Him to be
Shouldn't He reign over you and me?
Let Jesus be Lord, he's one who can't fail
He's the pep in your step - He's the wind in your sail

To heights yet known as only He can do
The harvest is ready but the laborers are few
We'll say one thing and even begin to pray
It's amazing how we still tend to go our own way
He said cast all your care for He cares for us
Why do we keep holding it and put up a fuss?
When He's made the way clear for us to prevail
The word says we're the head and not the tail

God has not given us the spirit of fear
But time after time and year after year
We'll try to figure out God and what He'll do now
It was not meant for our minds to know just how
Blessed is the one who makes the Lord His trust
Using faith as the key and obedience a must

Allow Jesus to be Lord and we'll never be the same
There's power in the blood and authority in His name.

Reflections

My thoughts are:

_____

_____

_____

_____

_____

_____

_____

Reflections

My thoughts are:

_____

_____

_____

_____

_____

_____

_____

Reflections

My thoughts are:

_____

_____

_____

_____

_____

_____

_____

Who are U?

Behold, what manner of love the Father hath bestowed upon us, that we should be called the Sons of God: therefore the world knoweth us not, because it knew him not.

(1Jn 3:1)

Do your surroundings, your culture or society dictate

Whose **U** are or who **U** are, or maybe "fate?"

Puts **U** in a place where you're not sure

Of what's right or wrong - a deceptive lure

To steer **U** in the way that pleases man

When actually **U** have delayed God's plan

Now He waits for **Us** to surrender our mind

To stop living this life as though you were blind

He's opened your eyes to what is hidden from some

He's given **U** liberty through His Son

But what do **U** do, **U** act as if

U don't have the power, hanging from a cliff

Hoping **U** don't fall cause after all

U don't know who **U** are !

15

You have something far more precious

than this world can give

The ability to die to self and still yet LIVE !!

He says give it away and it's multiplied back

That's not sensible - seems crazy in fact

Keep waving your banner when called to war

Don't just watch it fall to the floor

Who are **U**, who am **I?** Let's keep it real

We are redeemed from the curse

We are children of God

That's the deal.

Reflections

My thoughts are:

_____

_____

_____

_____

_____

_____

_____

_____

Reflections

My thoughts are:

_____

_____

_____

_____

_____

_____

_____

_____

Reflections

My thoughts are:

_____

_____

_____

_____

_____

_____

_____

Breaking the Enemy's Hold

What is your situation?

What is your circumstance?

Do you need to search deep within your spirit?

Or can you see it by taking a glance?

Satan wants what God wants - your body, mind and soul

If he gets his way he would have reached his goal

Many times it's not obvious but subtly detected

He poisons all that he touches and doesn't care if infected

The enemy has a hold that does not let go

Unless, you give it the Word by telling it NO!

You've got to know that what you say has power

So when you speak, speak with authority

Christ is your refuge and God - a strong tower

Action takes place the realm you don't see

When the Lord said this is your daily bread

Walk this every day with your feet shod

We can't relax in yesterday's food being fed

It's a new day, put on the **whole** armor of God

We already know we are in a spiritual battle

Time gives us an allotted span on this earth

Satan looks for that weak link in your life to rattle

So be secure in your worth:

You are a new creation, redeemed from the curse

Set free from condemnation, more than a conqueror,

joint heirs with Christ, light of the world, salt of the earth

reconciled with God, overtaken with blessings,

healed by the stripes of Jesus, an ambassador for Christ,

having the peace of God and given everlasting life!

Reflections

Does the enemy have a hold on me?

_____

_____

_____

_____

_____

_____

Reflections

Does the enemy have a hold on me?

_____

_____

_____

_____

_____

_____

Reflections

Does the enemy have a hold on me?

_____

_____

_____

_____

_____

_____

_____

Do you really know my voice?

My sheep know my voice, a stranger's they'll not obey
Whom will you serve, choose ye this day
How much time do you think you've got?
Less than you may realize - not a lot

I am everywhere - omnipresent, wherever you go
Is there anything done that I would not know?
Hold fast to your faith, surrender to Me
The essence of your being will be set free

Be true to yourself and seek My face
And I will speak to you in your hidden place
Certain things happen and you question Me, why?
I am not a man that I should lie

I am the door of which you must enter in
Don't be fooled thinking you can bring sin
Into My presence, cause I must turn away
Your destiny is planned, I'll show you the way

I want to reveal to you so much more
There is a fight for your soul and we are at war
Mirror, mirror on the wall
Will you answer when I call?
You are so precious, but I give you a choice
Ask yourself this, do I really know His voice?

Reflections

Can I hear His voice?

_____

_____

_____

_____

_____

_____

Reflections

Can I hear His voice?

_____

_____

_____

_____

_____

_____

Reflections

Can I hear His voice?

_____

_____

_____

_____

_____

_____

 Reflections

Can I hear His voice?

_____

_____

_____

_____

_____

_____

Be a Doer of the Word

Can you recall when you asked God to speak a word to your
heart?
And then you waited patiently for Him to impart
A portion of Himself, that's what you need
Now the question is, did you take heed?

He honored your request, now what did you do?
Remember His thoughts are from spiritual view
Well, it's not the answer you had expected
So now your mind tells you to reject it

Because of what He said, you let it fall to the side
Unwilling to let the Master be your guide
The challenge comes to our body and soul
Being victorious should be your goal

You've got to believe, you will prevail
Negative thinking will cause you to fail
Some won't yearn for more, no desire to pursue
But you can make great things happen, if only a few

Let's not be hearers only, sitting out on God
Saying Amen preacher, while we sit back and nod
We must keep moving to stay in this race
No sense in playing if you're content with first base

The time is right now while you still have breath
There's room on the boat, so don't get left!

Reflections

Am I a doer of the Word?

_____

_____

_____

_____

_____

_____

Reflections

Am I a doer of the Word?

_____

_____

_____

_____

_____

_____

Reflections

Am I a doer of the Word?

_____

_____

_____

_____

_____

_____

Reflections

Am I a doer of the Word?

_____

_____

_____

_____

_____

_____

_____

II

Mid Day Snack

"But the Lord said unto Samuel, Look not on his countenance, or on the height of his stature; because I have refused him: for the Lord seeth not as man seeth; for man looketh on the outward appearance, but the Lord looketh on the heart".

I Samuel 16:7 KJV

One Cup or Two?

What appears one way could indeed be another

Try loving your enemy and not just a sister or brother

There's a war for your soul on the left, on the right

It won't be won by your power or your might

Set before you are 2 cups one of which to drink

The choice you make is more serious than you think

You say that you'll follow me wherever you go

But some of my disciples even said - no!

My love goes beyond what you could ever conceive

If you will be led of My spirit and just believe

There is but one cup - only one to partake

And yes there is another, that decision you'll make

I watch over My people, I don't slumber nor sleep

I am God - I am truth, my promises I keep

Let it rain on you even when the sun is shining

I don't run by your clock, but I have perfect timing

The world is temporal using means to gain wealth

But I say to give away even more of yourself

My blessings flow abundantly - I have what you need

Deliverance, peace and joy making you free indeed.

Reflections

My thoughts are:

_____

_____

_____

_____

_____

_____

Reflections

My thoughts are:

_____

_____

_____

_____

_____

_____

Reflections

My thoughts are:

_____

_____

_____

_____

_____

_____

A Heart Condition

I just finished memorizing a verse in Matthew 6
About where my heart is, there my heart will be
That's a good one to know cause it's working for me.
Can't forget I Samuel 16, about the Lord looks on the heart
I like this one too, since I've been saved I fit that part

But one of my favorite verses is in Psalm 57
About my heart being fixed singing and giving praise
Hallelujah! Yes Lord, I'll shout all of my days
I believe I got this all under control
I'll say these scriptures and reach my goal
I want to go far with God and reap the benefits
I'm tired of everybody else getting what I should get

After all, I've been walking with God for years!!
I can't name many folks who have shed as many tears
That I have from things not going my way
Even thinking about it makes me pretty upset I'd say

God, do you hear me? Do you see me down here?
Cause I need your attention - you got to make things clear
I'm one of yours, been one of yours for a long time
And I see others being blessed but where's mine?
Well, I'll wait for my answer cause I need to know
Why Sis Sally reaps so much, and so does Brother Joe !!

Oh my goodness, what am I saying?
How on earth have I gotten to this point?
A still sweet voice spoke:
Before your parents were born, I chose you to anoint
Every breath you take cannot be done on your own
I kept a hedge of protection around much of the unknown
Even to you, because you were set apart
Before I can fill your cup, I had to first show you your heart.

Reflections

My heart is:

_____

_____

_____

_____

_____

_____

# Reflections

My heart is:

_____

_____

_____

_____

_____

_____

Reflections

My heart is:

_____

_____

_____

_____

_____

_____

 Reflections

My heart is:

_____

_____

_____

_____

_____

_____

Truth Stands

Will you ever sell the truth to gain the favor of men?
To win acceptance from others who have not been
Where Christ has taken you upon His wings
And set you high where angels sing

There's wisdom in truth - it can stand on it's own
Sometimes you might find it standing alone
Search for it diligently as buried treasure
For there's a reward which cannot be measured

God's word is certain and it can't be changed
To suit what we think needs to be arranged
And if you think that no one will know
It's being recorded, you reap what you sow

Carry the truth wherever you go
Speak it, live it, so others will know
To your character is noble and rooted firm
The blessings will follow and honor you've earned

All Christians should acknowledge that which is true
It's our testimony to all, the very least we can do.

# Reflections

What do I stand for?

_____

_____

_____

_____

_____

_____

_____

Reflections

What do I stand for?

_____

_____

_____

_____

_____

_____

Reflections

What do I stand for?

_____

_____

_____

_____

_____

_____

Unexpected

Out of the blue - unprepared - now what do I do?

To maintain my composure, I suppressed my feeling
When it seems like someone is actually stealing
All that I've planned in my own little world
Here it comes like it or not, it's already been hurled
In my direction, it's happening fast
Did anyone care or even bother to ask?
What do I think or how it effects me
I was given no choice, but simply to agree

Out of the blue - unprepared - now what do I do?

Let's put some thought into what's really going on
I'm not the only fish swimming in this pond
Maybe someone else was thrown the same curve ball
Perhaps they are trying to stand very tall
Dealing with issues that need to be addressed
I'm confident in knowing God will handle the rest

Out of the blue - unprepared - now what do I do?

Pastor George Evans said,
"change is inevitable if I want to progress"
I want to move forward and nothing less
Every occurrence is not without hope
See it as an opportunity to climb up the rope
What may seem to appear as being limited
Could very well work out for my benefit

Out of the blue - I'll now know what to do.

Reflections

My thoughts are:

_____

_____

_____

_____

_____

_____

_____

Reflections

My thoughts are:

_____

_____

_____

_____

_____

_____

Reflections

My thoughts are:

_____

_____

_____

_____

_____

_____

_____

For His Purpose

Your life was intentionally weaved in God's hands

The impact you hold could be as infinite as the sands

Your breath comes from Him of which no man can give

Unique in your own way He purposed you to live

Wondering about next year, even 5 years from now

Asking those questions of, why, when and how?

Let's think, is there really anything holding you back?

Or is it simply easier to mingle in the pack

If you are, it would take a relationship with the King

There's no doubt - He possesses everything

Single or married - it doesn't matter to Him

If you give Him permission, you can't help but win

Get excited! Be excited! He chose **you** in His plan

Your blueprint is distinctive because no one else can

Be as special as you are and wonderfully made

It's not about beauty or anything that could fade

The world distorts your view, but in Christ you are wise

So envision your purpose through your spiritual eyes

You'll need to execute faith on the journey you travel

At times it might get bumpy like going over gravel

Remember, you're on a mission so don't permit fear

To come in and disrupt the reason of why you are here.

 Reflections

My purpose is:

_____

_____

_____

_____

_____

_____

_____

Reflections

My purpose is:

_____

_____

_____

_____

_____

_____

_____

Reflections

My purpose is:

_____

_____

_____

_____

_____

_____

Reflections

My purpose is:

_____

_____

_____

_____

_____

_____

About my Fathers' Business

Have you ever felt like a stranger in this earth?
Asking, what's the purpose? What's my worth?
People meaning well saying,
here's what you should do.
While God waits patiently for us to tap into
The wonders of His kingdom, as only He
Can uncover our eyes - allowing us to see

We're the children of the Most High God!
What an awesome privilege that is
To know we're chosen to be one of His
But somehow I think we tend to forget
Labor in the Kingdom isn't over, not yet

Our work is continuous until Jesus returns
My Fathers' business is the primary concern
Do you want our King to come back finding you
With folded arms and nothing to do?
Inside each of us is placed a destiny
Full of potential, power and ability

When we commune with God the creator of all
Wisdom is summoned and answers the call
It's real and available to any man
Trust the Almighty - it's all in the plan
It isn't our agenda that carries us through
But to give to the Father and honor that's due.

 Reflections

My thoughts are:

_____

_____

_____

_____

_____

_____

Reflections

My thoughts are:

_____

_____

_____

_____

_____

_____

Reflections

My thoughts are:

_____

_____

_____

_____

_____

_____

III

Bedside Chat

"Wherefore God also hath highly exalted him, and given him a name which is above every name:

That at the name of Jesus every knee should bow, of things in heaven, and things in earth, and things under the earth;

And that every tongue should confess that Jesus Christ is Lord, to the glory of God the Father".

Philippians 2:9-11 KJV

Freedom from Chains

The weight that we carry, shouldn't be ours to keep
It holds us underwater, out in the deep
That we lose our breath, cause it's much too much
Blurring our focus, direction and such

The mind, will and emotions will try us each time
They'll have us thinking everything is fine
We know satan is out there - but is he always the one?
Who makes each decision when it's all said and done

What's holding you down, the thing you can't shake
You carry it around and perhaps keeps you awake
Think on it, seriously take a minute or two
Whatever it is has attached itself to you

It's the matter you'll dismiss each time it's revealed
So good you've earned a degree in keeping it concealed
You say you want to be free - totally freed indeed
You want a beautiful garden but you won't pluck the weeds

The chains you wear may be invisible to some
The areas we look over will begin feeling like a ton
Until you release it, it will keep coming back
It's imperative you stay on the right track

Go to God in your secret place
Address your issue face to face
Uncover yourself and simply be real
Standing, sitting or perhaps you may kneel

God will take your struggles, your burdens and concerns
When you truly let it go, He'll make sure it burns
Whew! what a relief - your shackles are broken
Finish your race, for the Lord has spoken

Reflections

Am I free?

_____

_____

_____

_____

_____

_____

 Reflections

Am I free?

_____

_____

_____

_____

_____

_____

Reflections

Am I free?

_____

_____

_____

_____

_____

_____

Reflections

Am I free?

_____

_____

_____

_____

_____

_____

_____

Daddy, I'm coming home!

I've allowed deception to come pluck me away

Piece by piece - a little each day

Sitting right beside me as a friend would

But whispering lies by telling me I could

Be happy and satisfied in so many ways

I deserve what pleases me - I've got lots of days

Falling for it, not at first - it took some time

Compromise came in and played with my mind

I'm so far away from righteousness in God's sight

While telling me to give in and surrender the fight

For someone else that may have been true

But somehow my spirit knew what to do

So I ran to my Father with all that I had

Laid at His feet and called Him, Dad

God was waiting for me with open arms

And change took place and I felt very warm

It seemed like the Son was shining on me

Then He smiled and said: Allow me

To complete in you what you were meant to be...

Reflections

My thoughts are:

_____

_____

_____

_____

_____

_____

Reflections

My thoughts are:

_____

_____

_____

_____

_____

_____

Reflections

My thoughts are:

_____

_____

_____

_____

_____

_____

_____

Now Stand

How does one have joy in the midst of a trial?
How does one have hope when soon it fades away?
Where does one get the strength to make it through?
You must speak to the mountain and <u>mean</u> what you say!

Not so enemy, you will not rob me of my right
To receive what is predestined on my flight
To reach beyond what is even in my sight
I'm strong in the Lord and in the power of His might

I choose, to invite the presence of my King
I will soar higher than the eagle's wing
He's my rock and my fortress, who will not fail
More reliable than the postman delivering my mail

Now stand, the Lord is pruning <u>you</u> from head to toe
In order to replenish, something has to go
He uses the fertilizer of which only He can provide
Just accept what He's doing with arms open wide

If you want more of Him, it's at your fingertips
But you'll have to verbalize it with your lips

So the next time you enter into a storm
And the way out may not be clear
Remember it is <u>not</u> an obstacle but an <u>opportunity</u>
Know God is your escape, He is always near.

Reflections

What am I standing for?

_____

_____

_____

_____

_____

_____

Reflections

What am I standing for?

_____

_____

_____

_____

_____

_____

Reflections

What am I standing for?

_____

_____

_____

_____

_____

_____

We are One

Here we are together, one in the Lord
Blessed with eternal life Christ has poured
How can we not rejoice when all has been done
For we have the blood of Jesus - God's own Son
Truly it's a blessing knowing everything is right
We can have peace with things in and out of sight
We need to hold onto the promises our God gave
His love made the difference that all may be saved.

Search our hearts Lord, for we're all a new creation
Bind us together, where there's no separation
In our lives, let's show love and compassion
Our eyes kept on Christ and following His fashion
Let us rejoice always, we're free you and me
Exercising our faith not limited to what we see
This is not our world, this is not our home
We are constantly traveling but never alone
United with Christ, we're heaven bound
All in an instant through a trumpet sound!

Reflections

My thoughts are:

_____

_____

_____

_____

_____

_____

Reflections

My thoughts are:

_____

_____

_____

_____

_____

_____

Reflections

My thoughts are:

_____

_____

_____

_____

_____

_____

To God be the Glory

Once I felt threatened - lost with uncertainty
But God reached down and set my soul free
All the pain, misery and strife
Was trying to deprive me of my future life

I made false accusations of which no one deserved
Not even knowing I was being reserved
God still claimed me through all these years
Through His infinite patience, he dried my tears

His majestic ordinance of Divine power
Able to touch billions in any given hour
Reaching and surpassing the ends of the earth
Knowing all about us even before birth

He cares for His people more than we know
He gives His word that we may grow
He teaches our hearts to be loving and kind
To develop our faith and secure our mind

To God be the glory, I solemnly exclaim
Always and forever exalting His name
God's word is as a harp playing a tune
While knowing that our Savoir is coming soon!

Reflections

My thoughts are:

_____

_____

_____

_____

_____

_____

Reflections

My thoughts are:

_____

_____

_____

_____

_____

_____

_____

 Reflections

My thoughts are:

_____

_____

_____

_____

_____

_____

_____

An Awesome God

Who else could design such a beautiful creation
From beginning to end and every generation
Who else has the ability to form the earth
Shaping mankind before there was birth

There's only one who could create such a vast universe
You can't fit Him in your wallet, nor can you a purse
He can't be bought nor can He be sold
He's everywhere, everyday, anytime, I'm told

If a person desired to know Him, they should
Ask him into their heart, for anyone could
He's the most truest love you'll ever know
It is a fact, not fiction, I know it to be so

There's detours and caution signs for your protection
Be glad He's leading in the right direction
You'll be on a journey, it may seem like a long ride
Remember He's with you - never leaving your side

God is the maker of all in all
The one who hurdles us over the wall
The one who helps us if we fall
Believe me He's awesome, He'll answer your call.

Reflections

My thoughts are:

_____

_____

_____

_____

_____

_____

_____

Reflections

My thoughts are:

_____

_____

_____

_____

_____

_____

_____

Reflections

My thoughts are:

_____

_____

_____

_____

_____

_____

_____

Reflections

My thoughts are:

_____

_____

_____

_____

_____

_____

His Kingdom, will have no end...

Our comprehension is limited to the King's full glory
He does have a beginning, but no ending to His story
No likeness has been or ever will be
He is absolute without doubt throughout eternity

To have walked with Him - <u>must have been Heavenly</u>
To have heard Him - <u>would have been Prime</u>
To have witnessed His miracles - <u>Indescribable</u>
But to **know** Him is - <u>Divine</u>

Jesus, just the mention of His name
Brings comfort and healing and soothes any pain
Of scars incurred in this circle of life
When the world seems brutal and cuts like a knife
God knew how it would be before Adam and Eve
How Lucifer would fall and begin to deceive
This one and that one - too many to name
All made choices but who takes the blame?

Praise God for Jesus, He is our hope
Not Budha, not Mohamed and not the Pope
His body was on loan to us for 33 years
Mary must have cried very special tears
Now His spirit lives on in the heart of those
Who've accepted His invitation and knows
The real meaning of life in Christ
Truly He was the ultimate sacrifice.

Reflections

My thoughts are:

_____

_____

_____

_____

_____

_____

Reflections

My thoughts are:

_____

_____

_____

_____

_____

_____

_____

Reflections

My thoughts are:

_____

_____

_____

_____

_____

_____

Reflections

My thoughts are:

_____

_____

_____

_____

_____

_____

IV

Munchies

"O taste and see that the Lord is good: Blessed is the man that trust in him".

Psalm 34:8 KJV

For you, Lord

I'm standing in a place where I only see you
All that my grandma told me was true

I'm remembering back to when she gave me your word
Trying to reach me and get my heart stirred

I'm drowning in fear cause I don't want to die
The end is near and my time draws nigh
I know it's you , Lord giving me courage to face
Whatever lies before me in this strange place

Oh how I remember what grandma spoke
I didn't write it down but I took mental notes

She praised and thanked you for all you've done
How we'd all perish if it weren't for God's Son

I wouldn't be "left" had I accepted your invitation
If I'd only asked Jesus into my heart,
I wouldn't be in this situation

Nevertheless, here I am - giving all that I have
I've done this to myself - I've chosen this path

I cannot let this world take me fully out
For you Lord, I'll finish this route
I'll leave this life with hope in my heart
Of seeing you Lord and never to part

I'll bow down before you giving glory to your name
To live with you forever is an absolute gain

Don't close the door Lord; is there a place for me?
It's an honor to die for you, I want to be free.

Reflections

My thoughts are:

_____

_____

_____

_____

_____

Reflections

My thoughts are:

_____

_____

_____

_____

_____

Reflections

My thoughts are:

_____

_____

_____

_____

_____

_____

Reflections

My thoughts are:

_____

_____

_____

_____

_____

_____

Somethin' Real

Graspin', graspin' for something
Lookin', lookin' for anything
People want a quick fix
A simple cure for what ails you
Young folks got all the answers
The older ones answer before you ask
You're comin' and goin' at the same time

Caught up in it? – not me, I'm just livin' it ya see
Gotta get here, gotta go there
Gotta say a quick prayer while I do my hair
Wait! Hold up – I need something real
Somethin' that will hold me
Perhaps even scold me
Yes, when I'm wrong
Thinkin' back to that ole song
My grandma sang when she cooked my meal
Somethin' with substance, somethin' real

My family, dear family can't give me what I long for
My friends, true friends can't do much more
I yearn to come over to the other side
Where I can allow God to be my guide
This world can't keep me – I long to be free
I'm shakin' loose the chains to enable me

To go on now, goin' up the road
Dropping the weight of my heavy load
I've gotta make a choice cause I know the deal
Time is
not promised
for somethin' real

Reflections

Real to me is:

_____

_____

_____

_____

_____

_____

Reflections

Real to me is:

_____

_____

_____

_____

_____

_____

Reflections

Real to me is:

_____

_____

_____

_____

_____

_____

Reflections

Real to me is:

_____

_____

_____

_____

_____

_____

Tis' the Season

Tis the season to be?
Jolly is what most people think of when they hear this.
Why does being jolly only apply to the Christmas season?
Wouldn't it be nice if folks were jolly all year round?
Let's focus on being joyful as a way of life. This valuable gift is a
heartfelt experience. Christmas is a day set aside to reflect on
Jesus' birth. Everyday is a blessing. Let's not get "wrapped" up
with everything else while missing out on the true meaning of life.

So it is, and what have I done?
Too much to do - I'm always on the run
No one really understands
That I can never finish my plans
My family needs this, my friends need that
I wonder how I keep my sanity in tact

Not to mention the household cleaning
Can anyone help? what's the meaning?
Both kids need braces
Finances are low
I have a little saved up
But soon that too will go

I have to attend a conference today at 4:30
This means of course I'll need to hurry
I won't have time to cook a good dinner
So I'll order a pizza, that's always a winner
Each day I'm being pulled on my left and right
I need time to exhale, can someone show me the light?

109

Reflections

What has me wrapped up?

_____

_____

_____

_____

_____

_____

Reflections

What has me wrapped up?

_____

_____

_____

_____

_____

_____

Reflections

What has me wrapped up?

_____

_____

_____

_____

_____

_____

Reflections

What has me wrapped up?

_____

_____

_____

_____

_____

_____

Flowing in the Spirit

Valerie Brown

Christian Poems à la carte

For additional copies of "*Flowing In The Spirit*", products or other books offered by Monarch Publications, LLC visit Monarch Publications, LLC website.

www.monarchpublicationsllc.webs.com

See additional books published by Monarch Publications, LLC

available on audio

See what others are saying about this dynamic publication;

"The heart issues that you describe are right on...All servants, even those who are leaders can benefit from preparing a heart to serve."

Dr. Rodney Swope

Rod & Staff Enterprises

www.rodnstaff.net

"WARNING: WHAT YOU ARE ABOUT TO READ MAY BE DANGEROUS TO YOUR SPIRTUAL AND POLITICAL HEALTH!"

Apostle Bennie Fluellen

Overflow Ministries Covenant Church

www.omccministries.com

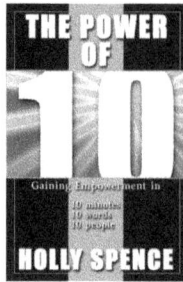

You've rendered an excellent program of empowerment. Very nicely done! Good flow. Nice overlaps between key topics. I especially liked the areas where you completely turn loose and throw the fire of your personality into it. That fire is "you" and makes the book. Very impressive methodology. Keep it up!

Larry Trujillo
Principal Consultant
Oracle Corporation

I think your book so far is well laid out, easy to read, interactive and engaging. Each chapter I've read, entices me to participate in the process and the activities. It's very applicable to life, not just work.

Cindy Dutra
Oracle Corporation

Workshops are currently being scheduled for corporate entry-level management, senior executives, church leadership and team workshops.

For workshop information and speaking engagement requests please send an email to

monarchpublcaitonsllc@yahoo.com

.

www.ingramcontent.com/pod-product-compliance
Lightning Source LLC
Chambersburg PA
CBHW031856090426
42741CB00005B/513